AND WAS AROUND WHILE I WAS ON
THIS JOURNEY. IT WAS A LOT OF
TEARS, HEARTACHE AND HEADACHE
(LOL) OF COURSE YOU KNOW
HOW MUCH I APPRECIATE YOUR
SUPPORT AS ONE OF THESE WAS
DEDICATED TO YOU (EVEN THOUGH
YOU DIDNT NOTICE UNTIL I
POINTED IT OUT TO YOU)

JUST THOUGHT YOU SHOULD KNOW

THANKS AS ALWAYS ALICIA!

— THOMAS
TRENH

TRIGGER WARNING

THIS BOOK TOUCHES ON THEMES OF SUICIDE, DEATH, SEXUAL
ASSAULT AND MENTAL HEALTH

ACKNOWLEDGEMENTS

THIS IS FOR YOU

YOU WILL ALWAYS HAVE A PLACE IN MY HEART

THANKS FOR BEING *YOU*

LIFE IS TOO REAL AT TIMES

AND WE KNOW LIFE IS HARD

HOW MANY TIMES DO WE HAVE TO HEAR THAT?

WE ALL EXPERIENCE IT IN DIFFERENT WAYS

I HAD ALWAYS THOUGHT THAT I WAS ALONE

AND THAT I WOULD ALWAYS BE — SUFFERING BY MYSELF

NO ONE WOULD UNDERSTAND ME

NOR WOULD ANYONE BE ABLE TO UNDERSTAND WHAT I'VE GONE
THROUGH

BUT MAYBE YOU'LL BE THE ONE TO UNDERSTAND

BECAUSE WE SHARE THE SAME EXPERIENCES

OR MAYBE YOU CARE ENOUGH TO TRY AND UNDERSTAND

I HAVE REPETITIVE THOUGHTS AND THAT'S INTENTIONAL
BECAUSE FEELINGS LIKE THESE DON'T JUST COME AND GO
THEY POP UP IN MY MIND AND THEY MADE A HOME
IN THE CREVICES OF MY BRAIN
HAUNTING ME
WHEN I'M HAPPY OR WHEN I'M SAD

YOU KNOW I'M HURTING
RIGHT?
BUT I'M OK
I ALWAYS HAVE BEEN

AND YOU,
JUST KNOW
THAT YOU'LL BE OK TOO

THERE MAY OR MAY NOT BE A HAPPY ENDING

TO THIS STORY

NOT EVERYONE CAN LIVE HAPPY LIVES

NOT EVERYONE HAS THIS MAGICAL TURNING POINT

IN THEIR LIFE

OR THIS REALIZATION THAT EVERYTHING GETS BETTER

SOME PEOPLE DWELL

AND CAN'T MOVE ON

I CAN'T HELP MYSELF

I'M SORRY

BUT HERE IS MY STORY

MAYBE OURS HAVE CROSSED PATHS

DIFFERENT

I WAS DIFFERENT
AND I GUESS PEOPLE WERE AFRAID OF THAT
SO THEY ABUSED ME
I HOPE THOSE PEOPLE CAN CONTINUE
LIVING THEIR CAREFREE LIVES
KNOWING THEY HAVE BROKEN ME

CAREFREE

I DON'T REMEMBER MUCH OF MY PAST
CAREFREE DAYS AS A KID?
NOTHING TO WORRY ABOUT?
ALL I REMEMBER ARE THE BULLIES
WHO HURT ME EVERYDAY

I WAS SCARED
SCARED OF GOING BACK
I THOUGHT I COULD TRUST
MY FRIENDS
MY FAMILY

BUT I WAS WRONG
I DON'T MISS THE OLD DAYS
I COULDN'T LIVE AS A KID
CAREFREE

CHANGE

I TRIED CHANGING WHO I WAS
SO MAYBE I COULD FIT IN
BUT SOON YOU'LL REALIZE
THAT YOU CAN'T CHANGE
WHO YOU REALLY ARE

DISAPPOINTMENT

THE LOOK OF DISAPPOINTMENT
ON YOUR FACE
WHEN I DID SOMETHING
YOU DIDN'T APPROVE OF

SOMETHING THAT I HATE SEEING
SOMETHING THAT I CAN NEVER FORGET

BUT LITTLE DO YOU KNOW
I WAS A DISAPPOINTMENT
FROM THE MOMENT I WAS BORN

SELFISH

WHY DIDN'T YOU HELP ME?
I THOUGHT WE WERE FRIENDS

I DON'T WANT TO BE BULLIED TOO

SO YOU'D RATHER SEE ME SUFFER
ALONE
EVEN THOUGH YOU KNEW
I'D ALWAYS HAVE YOUR BACK
THIS WORLD – PEOPLE WILL ONLY DO THINGS
THAT BENEFIT THEMSELVES

<u>ELEMENTARY</u>

I DON'T REMEMBER MUCH OF MY PAST
BUT WHAT I DO HAUNTS ME
TIMES I WOULD GET PUNCHED
PUSHED AROUND
MADE FUN OF
SITTING ALONE AT THE LUNCH TABLE
WALKING AIMLESSLY DURING RECESS
ALONE
I WAS SCARED
BECAUSE I HAD NO ONE

PROVE

I'M BEING BULLIED
BECAUSE I'M BEING MYSELF

THEN PROVE THEM OTHERWISE

BUT WHAT DO I NEED TO PROVE
TO THE PEOPLE WHO DON'T MATTER?

CHILDHOOD THOUGHTS

WHAT IF
I JUST DISAPPEARED
FROM THIS WORLD
WOULD ANYONE
MISS ME?

<u>TERRIFIED</u>

THOUGHTS OF SUICIDE
MUST BE SCARY TO THINK ABOUT
IMAGINE HOW SCARED I AM
TO HAVE CONSTANTLY THOUGHT ABOUT IT
I CAN'T HELP IT
I CAN'T STOP THINKING ABOUT IT
AND I'M TERRIFIED
THAT I MIGHT GO THROUGH WITH IT

LOST

IT'S NOT WHAT I HAVE
OR DON'T HAVE
IT'S WHAT I'VE LOST

<u>SAFE HAVEN</u>

HOME WAS A SAFE HAVEN FOR ME
PROTECTION AGAINST THE CONSTANT TORMENT
SPACE TO REPOLISH AND REBUILD WORN DOWN ARMOR
THAT WAS BORN WITH THE NAÏVE

BUT MY HAVEN CRUMBLED
WHY AM I BEING BULLIED HERE?
IF I'M NOT SAFE HERE
WHERE IS MY SAFE HAVEN?

SUMMER NIGHTS

THE NIGHTS I CRIED MYSELF TO SLEEP
THE SUMMERS I WISHED WOULD NEVER END
I WAS SO SCARED
OF GOING BACK
TO EXPERIENCE IT ALL
OVER AGAIN

<u>A MAN</u>

YOUR STRENGTH
IS WHAT MAKES YOU A MAN

BUT I'VE BEEN BEATEN DOWN
UNTIL I WAS RAW AND WEAK
WHAT DOES THAT MAKE ME?

FORGIVE

I COULD FORGIVE
THOSE WHO HAVE HURT ME
BUT I WILL *NEVER* FORGET

TEENAGE THOUGHTS

YOU DON'T HAVE TO DO IT
DON'T KILL YOURSELF

JOKER

CAUSING LAUGHTER
I THOUGHT I WAS THE JOKER
BUT INSTEAD I WAS THE FOOL
AND I WAS A JOKE

BRAINWASHED

I HAD TO BRAINWASH MYSELF
AND MY OWN THOUGHTS –
THAT I HAD SOMETHING TO LIVE FOR
AND THAT TAKING MY OWN LIFE
WOULD JUST BE TAKING OPPORTUNITIES AWAY
FROM MYSELF
BECAUSE NO ONE ELSE KNEW THE PAIN I WAS IN
NO ONE EVER CARED TO KNOW
ISN'T THAT SAD?

STONE COLD

I'VE BEEN TOLD
I WAS DIFFICULT TO APPROACH
THAT I WAS A CHALLENGE TO READ
I'VE ALWAYS WONDERED WHY TOO

IT'S NOT FAIR FOR ME
TO PRESENT MYSELF THIS WAY
IS IT?

I AM THIS WAY-
HARD AND STONE COLD
BECAUSE I WOULD HAVE NEVER SURVIVED
IF I WASN'T THIS WAY

JUMP

IT FELT AS IF
YOU FOLLOWED ME HOME
THE SOUND OF ROCKS CLATTERING BY MY FEET
THEY HIT MY BACK, MY LEGS

AND WITH YOUR FRIENDS
YOU JUST COULDN'T HELP THE SHIT
FROM COMING OUT OF YOUR MOUTH
HUNGRY FOR MY REACTION

BUT WHAT I REMEMBER MOST
IN THAT MOMENT
WAS PRAYING
THAT YOU WOULDN'T END UP JUMPING ME

RUINED

TO MY BULLIES
I'VE ALWAYS WANTED TO KNOW
WHY YOU DID AND SAID SUCH CRUEL THINGS
BUT YOU'VE PROBABLY MOVED ON
NOT EVEN GIVING WHAT YOU DID TO ME
A SECOND THOUGHT
BUT I CAN'T MOVE ON THAT FAST
MY LIFE WAS RUINED
AND I'LL NEVER BE THE SAME
BECAUSE YOU HAVE BROKEN ME

AWAKE

I WOULD LIE AWAKE
FOR HOURS
I COULDN'T SLEEP
BECAUSE I WAS AFRAID

I KNEW THAT A NEW DAY
WOULD JUST BE LIKE ANY OTHER
BEING PUSHED AROUND
AND CALLED NAMES

THE ONLY WAY FOR ME
TO FALL ASLEEP
WAS TO TIRE MYSELF OUT
CRYING

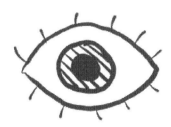

PARALYSIS

I LOOK AT YOU

AND YOU LOOK AT ME

WE BOTH SMILE

I'M HAPPY BECAUSE WE'RE SPENDING TIME TOGETHER

BUT THEN YOU PUSH ME DOWN

YOUR HANDS WRAPPED AROUND MY WRISTS

YOU'RE HURTING ME

I'M NO LONGER SMILING

I'M STRUGGLING – KICKING AND SCREAMING

BUT NOTHING COMES OUT OF MY MOUTH

I REALIZE I'M ASLEEP

I KEEP TELLING MYSELF TO WAKE UP

BUT I CAN'T

AFTER WHAT FEELS LIKE AN ETERNITY

I WAKE UP

GASPING FOR AIR

<u>NO EYES, EARS, NOSE, MOUTH, OR FEELINGS</u>

YOUR BREATH ON MY NECK
JUST BELOW MY EAR
WEIGHS ME DOWN
TURNS ME TO STONE
FROZEN IN TIME

NOT EVEN A BREATH ESCAPES MY MOUTH

IN THIS MOMENT
I DON'T WANT TO SEE YOU
I DON'T WANT TO HEAR YOU
I DON'T WANT TO SMELL YOU
I DON'T WANT TO TASTE YOU
I DON'T WANT TO FEEL YOU
I DON'T...
WANT TO BE ALIVE

YOU'LL NEVER FORGET

YOUR HAND WANDERED DOWN
AS IF IT WERE A PASSAGE INTO MY BRAIN
BECAUSE YOU BROKE IN
CAUSED ME TO FEAR – BE AFRAID

THE SMIRK ON YOUR FACE
EVIL, MENACING
AN IMAGE FOREVER BURNED
IN MY MIND

THE LOOK OF PLEASURE
ALL OVER YOUR FACE
WAS JUST AGONY
WRITTEN ALL OVER MINE

YOU USED ME
PLAYED WITH ME
LEFT ME
DISGUSTED WITH MYSELF

MD

I TRIED TO EXPLAIN TO YOU
THAT I WAS NOT OK
AND THAT I WAS STRUGGLING
BUT YOU COULDN'T UNDERSTAND
AND INSTEAD
YOU CHOOSE TO BLAME ME
FOR WHY THINGS
ARE THE WAY THEY ARE
GOOD LUCK
SAVING PEOPLE WHO REALLY NEED YOU
BECAUSE YOU KILLED ME

MY APOLOGIES

I'M SORRY I COULDN'T TELL YOU
I WASN'T ABLE GET OUT OF MY BED
I NEVER WANTED TO LEAVE THE HOUSE
I DIDN'T HAVE THE STOMACH TO EAT

I'M SORRY I COULDN'T TELL YOU
I HATED EVERYTHING ABOUT ME
I COULDN'T EVEN FACE MYSELF
I DIDN'T WANT ANYONE TO SEE ME LIKE THIS

I'M SORRY I COULDN'T TELL YOU
I WAS STRUGGLING WITH MY MENTAL HEALTH
I WAS DEPRESSED
I WANTED TO KILL MYSELF

AND I'M SORRY TO MYSELF
FOR THINKING THAT I EVER OWED YOU ANYTHING
WHEN YOU WERE NEVER THERE
I DON'T OWE YOU ONE THING

UNILATERAL

DOES IT MATTER
THAT WE WERE FRIENDS FOR YEARS
YOU TURNED YOUR BACK ON ME
ALL THAT WE BUILT TOGETHER
CRUMBLED INTO NOTHINGNESS
AS I DROPPED YOU OUT OF MY LIFE
TOO DAMN FAST
BECAUSE IN THE BACK OF MY MIND
I KNEW YOU COULDN'T BE TRUSTED
I EVEN TOLD YOU
AND YOU PROVED ME RIGHT

THIRD CHANCES

I SHOULD EXPLAIN MYSELF
IS A THOUGHT I CONSTANTLY HAVE
BUT WHY SHOULD I?
THIS ISN'T THE FIRST TIME
I ALREADY GAVE YOU ANOTHER CHANCE
YOU DON'T DESERVE ME
I DON'T DESERVE THIS

XX

WHEN I TRY TO HIDE MY SCARS
WITH A LAUGH
DOES ANYONE NOTICE?

WHEN I TRY TO HIDE MY TEARS
WITH A SMILE
DOES ANYONE NOTICE?

DID ANYONE NOTICE
MY CRY FOR HELP
WHEN I JUST SAT IN SILENCE?

#WHYWESTAYSILENT

HOW CAN A MAN BE ABUSED?
HOW CAN A MAN BE SEXUALLY ASSASULTED?
HOW CAN A MAN BE RAPED?
MEN BEING SEXUALLY ASSAULTED? THAT'S A JOKE, RIGHT?

ARE YOU GOING TO ASK ME WHAT I WAS WEARING?
ARE YOU GOING TO ASK ME WHY DIDN'T I JUST STOP HIM?
ARE YOU GOING TO ASK ME WHY I DIDN'T
OR COULDN'T PROTECT MYSELF?

SHAME, RIDICULE, DISBELIEF...
BECAUSE I DON'T NEED TO BE ACCUSED
OF BEING TOO WEAK-
ACCUSED OF BEING LESS THAN

DROWNING

IMAGINE BEING TOSSED INTO THE MIDDLE OF AN OCEAN
TOLD TO SURVIVE
BUT YOU DON'T KNOW HOW TO SWIM
YOU MIGHT BE ABLE TO STAY AFLOAT
BUT HOW LONG UNTIL YOUR BODY WEARS OUT?
AND YOU DON'T HAVE THE STRENGTH ANYMORE
YOU DROWN
YOUR LUNGS BEGIN TO FILL WITH WATER
NOW YOU'RE JUST WAITING TO DIE
SLOW AND PAINFUL

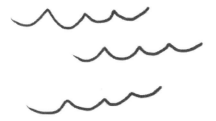

FOOL

SOMETIMES I WONDER

WHY YOU LIKE TO PLAY GAMES WITH ME

DO YOU EVEN REALIZE IT?

BUT NO MATTER HOW MANY TIMES

I GET PLAYED BY YOU

I CONTINUE TO SMILE

BECAUSE I TRUST YOU

AND NO MATTER HOW MANY MORE TIMES YOU PLAY ME

UNTIL YOU TELL ME

I'LL CONTINUE TO PLAY THE FOOL

WORRY

I CAN SEE PAST THE LIGHT
THAT'S EMINATING FROM THE FIRE BURNING
FAR BEYOND THE BACKS YOUR EYES
I CAN'T LIE AND SAY IT WAS A SURPRISE
SEEING THE HURT HIDDEN BENEATH THE SHADOWS

WHILE PEOPLE ARE CAPTIVATED
BY THE SPARKLES OF YOUR EYES
I KNOW THE FACE YOU HAVE ON IS ONLY A LIE
TO REDIRECT THEM FROM YOUR TRUTH
AND I CAN'T HELP BUT WORRY

DON'T CROSS THE LINE

YOU KNOW THAT FEELING
WHEN YOU'RE TEETERING ON THAT LINE
WONDERING IF YOU SHOULD CROSS IT OR NOT

THAT FEELING OF
WHEN YOU'RE ABOUT TO PUNCH SOMEONE
WHEN YOU'RE ABOUT TO BURST OUT LAUGHING
WHEN YOU'RE ABOUT TO CRY

SOMETIMES
I'M STILL ON THAT LINE
ON WHETHER OR NOT I SHOULD TAKE MY OWN LIFE

PLAYED

I WAS STRUGGLING

SUFFERING

YOU PLAYED ME SO WELL

I BROKE

AT LEAST YOU WON'T GET TO PLAY ME

AND BREAK ME AGAIN

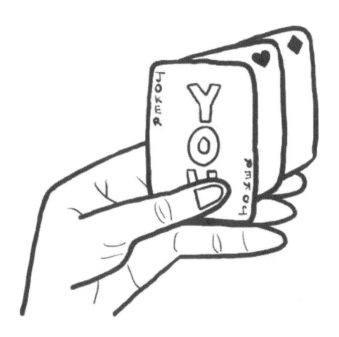

SCARED

WHEN YOU GET CAUGHT
IN A SITUATION OF LIFE OR DEATH
YOUR LIFE FLASHES BEFORE YOUR EYES
MOMENTS FOREVER BURNED
IN THE DEEPEST PARTS OF YOUR BRAIN

IMAGINE LIVING IN A WORLD
WHERE YOU'RE JUST *NOT* OK
KNOWING LIFE OR DEATH
LIKE THE MORNING KNOWS SUNRISE
EXPERIENCES OFTEN FREQUENTED

I USED TO BE SCARED
BUT NOT ANYMORE
IT DOESN'T PHASE ME
AND THAT
IS WHAT SCARES ME

<u>DISAPPEAR</u>

I THINK WE WERE BOTH THE SAME
IN MANY WAYS
WE FELT COMFORTABLE OPENING UP
BOTH STRUGGLING AND USED
I TRUSTED YOU
BUT YOU JUST DUMPED YOUR EMOTIONAL BAGGAGE ON ME
AND THEN DISAPPEARED
WHEN I NEEDED YOU
I THOUGHT I COULD TRUST YOU
BUT AS I THOUGHT
I WAS WRONG
I CAN'T TRUST ANYONE

MENTAL

THE GLARE OF THE SUN

ON TOP OF THE WATER

I STRETCH MY HAND

TO TRY AND REACH

THE SURFACE OF THE WATER

BUT I CAN'T SEEM TO GET ANY CLOSER

IT'S NOT THAT I'M NOT TRYING

PHYSICALLY

I JUST

CAN'T

MISSING

NO MATTER WHO IT IS I TALK TO, THERE'S ALWAYS A LIE USED TO
MANIPULATE MY EMOTIONS. THAT'S WHY I'M CRYING.
I WANT TO PUT A LITTLE FAITH, A LITTLE TRUST IN PEOPLE BUT I
ALWAYS END UP GETTING STABBED IN THE BACK. THAT'S WHY I'M
CRYING.
WHEN BORN INTO THIS WORLD, WITH MY SHIELD BEING MY
NAIVETY, IT WAS SHATTED BY EVIL INTENTIONS PEOPLE HAD
WHEN THEY TOOK ADVANTAGE OF ME. THAT'S WHY I'M CRYING.
I'M CRYING BECAUSE PIECES OF ME WERE TAKEN, STOLEN, RIPPED
FROM MY BODY AND I'VE LOST WHO I USED TO BE – THAT
PERSON WILL NEVER BE FOUND AGAIN.

<u>REMEMBER</u>

WHEN I HURT
ALL I CAN DO IS CRY
I'M CONSTANTLY BEING HURT
SO I'M CONSTANTLY CRYING

WHAT HAPPENS WHEN YOU HURT SO MUCH
YOU DON'T CRY ANYMORE
YOU DON'T KNOW HOW IT FEELS TO HURT
NOT ANYMORE

JUST SO YOU REMEMBER
HOW IT FEELS
PHYSICAL PAIN
STILL HURTS THE WAY YOU REMEMBER IT

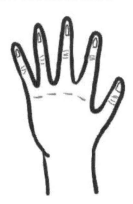

GO BACK

I SMILE
BECAUSE I'M HAPPY
BUT THEN I REMEMBER

THE LIES
BROKEN PROMISES
NEGATIVE EXPERIENCES
SWIRLING IN MY HEAD

I STOP SMILING
AND I FALL DEEPER
IN SOME DARK PLACE
I CAN'T HELP IT

WHY AM I EVEN HERE?
WHY AM I SMILING?
I WANT TO GO HOME

DEAD

PEOPLE HAVE ASKED ME
WHY ARE YOU SAD?
WHY DON'T YOU SMILE?
HOW DO I EVEN ANSWER?
I DON'T KNOW WHERE TO BEGIN

I'M BROKEN
THAT'S WHY
I TRY TO REMEMBER HOW IT FEELS
WHAT HAPPY FEELS LIKE
BUT I DON'T REMEMBER
I'M DEAD INSIDE

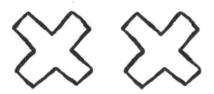

BREAKDOWN

WHY AM I AFRAID OF
THE FEELINGS I CONSTANTLY FEEL
PAIN, CONFUSION, STRESS, LONELINESS
I FEAR THOSE FEELINGS
BECAUSE IN THOSE MOMENTS
THAT I KNOW MUCH TO WELL
I WANT TO BREAKDOWN
BECAUSE I SEE NO END
AND I DON'T WANT TO BELIEVE
THAT THIS IS JUST HOW IT IS
BUT... THIS *IS* MY LIFE

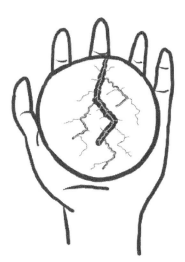

FALL PT. I

MY EYES ARE CLOSED
I FEEL A SLIGHT COOL BREEZE
A HAND RESTS ON MY BACK
IT FEELS COMFORTING
I TAKE A BREATH AND OPEN MY EYES
I'M STANDING ON THE EDGE
OF A DARK, ENDLESS HOLE

FALL PT. II

I FEEL PRESSURE ON MY BACK
I LOSE MY BALANCE AND BEGIN TO FALL
MY HEART BECOMES UNEASY
I SWING MY HANDS AROUND
HOPING TO GET A HOLD OF SOMETHING
SOMETHING THAT WILL SLOW ME DOWN
OR EVEN STOP ME
BUT AS I CONTINUE TO FALL
AND FALL
I HAVE NO HOPE OF SLOWING DOWN
MY HEART IS NO LONGER UNEASY
ALL I HAVE IS ONE THOUGHT
WHEN WILL I HIT THE BOTTOM?

BROKEN

MY HEART IS NOT JUST BROKEN
IT SHATTERED

YOU CAN TRY PICKING UP THE PIECES
AND PUTTING IT BACK TOGETHER AGAIN
BUT IT'LL NEVER BE THE SAME

HOW TO FEEL

I REALLY DONT WANT TO BE
THE BROKEN RECORD THAT KEEPS REPEATING
I WAS ABUSED, I WAS BROKEN
ITS CALLS FOR SOMEONE TO NOTICE
FOR SOMEONE TO VALIDATE MY FEELINGS
BUT I AM AND I DO
IT CONSTANTLY PLAYS IN MY HEAD
BECAUSE WHEN YOU'VE BEEN HURT
AGAIN AND AGAIN
YOU DON'T KNOW HOW TO FEEL ANYMORE
EVEN IN THE MOMENTS OF SMILE AND LAUGHTER
NO ONE BOTHERED TO REALIZE
THE RECORD WAS STILL BROKEN
SO IT'LL ALWAYS SKIP BACK TO
I WAS ABUSED, I WAS BROKEN
IS IT MY FAULT
THAT I KEEP THINKING OF THE WORST?
I CAN'T HELP MYSELF
I WAS ABUSED, I WAS BROKEN

AFRAID

WHAT ARE YOU AFRAID OF?
THE DARK?
INSECTS?
HEIGHTS?
NO.
I'M AFRAID OF GETTING HURT

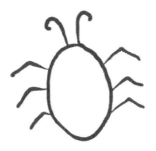

DESERVE

"YOU GET WHAT YOU DESERVE."

PEOPLE BACKSTABBING ME

LOSING TRUST IN EVERYONE

LIFE DOESN'T SEEM TO BE GETTING ANY BETTER

SHOULD I STILL BE HOPEFUL?

I GUESS I DESERVE IT

TO BE CONSTANTLY HURT

YOU'RE RIGHT

I DESERVE ALL THIS

HEART

YOU KNOW THE PAIN YOU FEEL
WHEN YOUR HEART IS HURTING
WHILE YOU'RE CRYING UNCONTROLLABLY

YOU FEEL THE PAIN DEEP INSIDE
THE PRESSURE THAT'S SQUEEZING YOUR HEART
IT WANTS TO BURST

IT FEELS LIKE YOUR HEART
IS ABOUT TO DROP
INTO YOUR STOMACH

TRAPPED

I'M TRAPPED BY MY OWN MIND
TO THINK I'M ALONE
AND THAT I'LL ALWAYS BE
BECAUSE THERE'S NO ONE I CAN TRUST
I CAN'T ALWAYS SEE
THE PEOPLE THAT ARE THERE FOR ME
THAT LINE HAS BEEN BLURRED
I'M SORRY
TO THOSE THAT CARE
AND THOSE THAT WERE THERE FOR ME
I'M SORRY

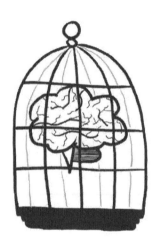

ABUSED

MY HEART ACHES

AND I DON'T KNOW WHY

MAYBE IT'S BECAUSE OF THE SWORDS

THAT'VE BEEN LUNGED INTO MY HEART

BACKSTABBED, LIED TO

OR MAYBE IT'S BECAUSE

ITS BEEN PLAYED WITH

AND ABUSED

LOOKING

I'M ALWAYS LOOKING
FOR SOMEONE TO CARE
FOR SOMEONE *WHO* CARES
BECAUSE I FEEL ALONE
BUT THE MORE I LOOK
THE LONELIER I FEEL

WHO AM I

YOU KNOW THAT POINT
WHEN YOU REALIZE
NOTHING IS GOING TO GO YOUR WAY
NOTHING IS WORKING OUT
THAT'S WHEN I GIVE UP
AND START TO LOSE MYSELF
OR WHO I USED TO BE

NOTHING WORKS OUT

THERE COMES A POINT
WHEN YOU REALIZE THAT YOU'VE DISAPPOINTED YOUR FAMILY
WITHOUT THEM HAVING TO SAY A SINGLE WORD
AND WITHOUT THEM EVEN KNOWING HOW

THERE COMES A POINT
WHEN YOU'VE BEEN DISAPPOINTED BY YOUR FAMILY
BECAUSE THERE'S NO WAY THEY COULD EVER UNDERSTAND THE
PAIN YOU'VE BEEN THROUGH
AND YOU DON'T EXPECT THEM TO UNDERSTAND BUT YOU'D
HOPE THEY WOULD TRY

THERE COMES A POINT
WHEN YOUR FRIENDS HAVE DISAPPOINTED YOU
IN MORE WAYS THAN ONE
AS IT WASN'T EASY FOR YOU TO GIVE YOUR TRUST
ONLY TO HAVE THEM BREAK IT

THERE COMES A POINT
WHEN THE WORLD HAS DISAPPOINTED YOU
NO ONE CARES ABOUT YOU
AND NO ONE EVER WILL
JUST GIVE UP

<u>ME</u>

THERE HAS ONLY EVER BEEN
ONE PERSON THERE FOR ME
THROUGH THE UPS AND DOWNS
AND THE TIMES I'VE PLUMMETED FACE FIRST
DOWN THE DEEPEST AND DARKEST HOLES

THE TIMES I'VE CRIED
AND WHEN MY HEART ACHED SO MUCH
I COULD FEEL THE PRESSURE
SQUEEZING MY HEART

THE ONLY PERSON
THAT I COULD EVER TRUST
ME

<u>DREAMS</u>

EVEN AS I CLOSE MY EYES
AND FALL IN A DEEP SLEEP
MY MEMORIES STILL HAUNT ME
WITH NIGHTMARES

I'M ALWAYS RUNNING AWAY
MY LEGS WOULD GIVE OUT
BUT I KNEW I COULDN'T STOP
I'D USE MY HANDS
DIGGING MY FINGERS INTO THE GROUND
TO HELP PULL ME FORWARD
MY FINGERNAILS COVERED IN DIRT
MY HANDS STAINED WITH BLOOD

I DON'T KNOW WHEN
I'LL STOP RUNNING AWAY
I'M TOO SCARED

DREAMS PT. II

AS I RUN
I DON'T BREAK MY STRIDE
NOT EVEN FOR ONE SECOND
TO SEE WHAT IT IS
I'M RUNNING FROM
BECAUSE I'M AFRAID
IT MIGHT JUST BE ME

PESSIMIST

NO MATTER HOW MANY TIMES
I TELL MYSELF
TO JUST DO SOMETHING
I END UP BACKING OUT

MY MIND
WOULD'VE ALREADY COME UP WITH
EVERYTHING THAT COULD GO WRONG
I CAN'T HELP IT

NEGATIVE

SOMETIMES I'LL PLAY A SCENARIO
HUNDREDS OF TIMES IN MY HEAD
OVER AND OVER AND OVER AND OVER
THINKING OF EVERY POSSIBLE OUTCOME
BECAUSE I DON'T WANT TO BE LET DOWN

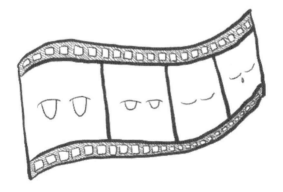

EYES

MY EYES WANDER AS WE TALK
BECAUSE I'M AFRAID
YOU'LL DISCOVER MY TRUTH
ALL THE PAIN
THAT HIDES WITHIN MY EYES

SECRETS

I DON'T KNOW
IF KEEPING SECRETS
TO MYSELF
IS HELPING ME
OR HURTING ME

RISK

RISKS USUALLY COME WITH EXTREME HIGHS OR EXTREME LOWS
AND EITHER WILL CHANGE YOUR LIFE DRASTICALLY

MY RISK IS TRUSTING IN YOU
I CUT OPEN ALL THE SCARS THAT HAD LEFT DEEP GASHES
REMEMBERING ALL THE PAIN
WHICH TOOK YEARS FOR ME TO MEND

JUST TO SHOW YOU
HOW REAL I WAS
HOW GENUINE I WAS
HOW MUCH PAIN I'VE BEEN THROUGH
HOW HONEST AND RAW I COULD BE

I LIKE RISKS
BUT THE ONLY HIGH I GET FROM THIS RISK
IS A MUTUAL RELATIONSHIP
IN CONTRAST TO THE LOW I'VE PLACED ON THIS BET
BEING LEFT WITH OPEN SCARS WHICH WILL TAKE YEARS
TO MEND AGAIN

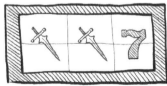

BLACKHOLE

YOU ALWAYS FALL BACK
ON THIS FEELING
AND NO MATTER HOW HARD
YOU TRY TO ESCAPE
YOU ARE PULLED BACK IN
THE THING IS
IT IS POSSIBLE TO LEAVE
BUT ONCE YOU FALL
BENEATH THE HORIZON
IT'S LIKE A BLACKHOLE
THERE IS NO ESCAPE

PRETEND

WHY IS IT THAT I FEEL BAD
FOR NOT BEING HAPPY
IT'S LIKE I OWE IT TO OTHERS
TO BE HAPPY
BUT IT GETS HARDER
YOU KNOW
PRETENDING TO BE OK

ALIVE

WAS IT BACK IN GRADE SCHOOL, WHEN YOU WERE RIDICULED ALMOST EVERYDAY/UNTIL THE POINT YOU ACTUALLY FEARED GOING TO SCHOOL BECAUSE IT HAD BECOME A ROUTINE/ TEACHERS DIDN'T CARE, YOUR *FRIENDS* DIDN'T EITHER AND YOUR PARENTS WOULDN'T UNDERSTAND/WAS THAT WHEN YOU DIED?

WAS IT BACK IN MIDDLE SCHOOL, WHEN YOU WERE SEXUALLY ASSAULTED BY SOMEONE YOU DIDN'T KNOW/AND AT THAT TIME YOU COULDN'T INTERPRET WHAT WAS JUST DONE BUT YOU FELT DISGUSTED/YOU HAD GONE HOME TRYING TO SCRUB THE GUILT OFF BUT COULDN'T/WAS THAT WHEN YOU DIED?

WAS IT BACK IN HIGH SCHOOL WHEN YOU THOUGHT THIS MOVE WOULD BE A BRAND NEW START/ONLY TO HAVE YOUR OLD EXPERIENCES FOLLOW YOU AND HAUNT YOU/TO THE POINT YOU THOUGHT THE ONLY WAY TO GET RID OF IT WAS DEATH/WAS THAT WHEN YOU DIED?

WAS IT BACK IN UNIVERSITY WHEN YOU WERE SEXUALLY ASSAULTED AGAIN/YOU COULDN'T OVERCOME THEIR STRENGTH BUT THOUGHT YOU WERE LUCKY TO STILL BE ABLE TO THINK STRAIGHT/WAS THAT WHEN YOU DIED?

I DIED
YEARS AGO

EXCUSES

I'M SCARED
BECAUSE OF THE THINGS I'VE BEEN THROUGH
AFRAID OF EXPERIENCING IT ALL AGAIN
OR COULD IT BE I'M JUST MAKING EXCUSES
FOR BEING THE WAY THAT I AM
EVEN I DOUBT MYSELF
TALKING MYSELF DOWN
AS IF MY EXPERIENCES WERE NOTHING

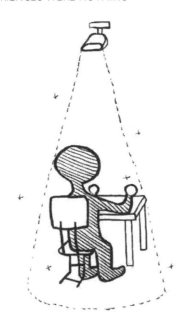

MASK

IT'S EASY FOR ME
TO PUT ON A BRAVE FACE
BUT I'M SUFFERING ON THE INSIDE
THE SADNESS EATS AWAY AT ME
MORE AND MORE EVERYDAY
BECAUSE I DON'T WANT PEOPLE TO KNOW
HOW DAMAGED I AM

PIERCED

I LIE AWAKE

A SPEAR PIERCED THROUGH MY BODY

RIGHT THROUGH MY HEART

FEELING THE WARMTH OF MY BLOOD

HEAT MY BODY AS IT SATURATES MY SHIRT

ALL I CAN DO IS WATCH THE CRIMSON BLOOD

DRIP DOWN OFF MY FINGERS

ONTO THE GROUND BELOW

AS MY ARMS AND LEGS DANGLE IN THE SKY

EXPECT

YOU KNOW WHAT'S FUNNY
ABOUT CONSTANTLY BEING BACKSTABBED
YOU DON'T REALLY GIVE A FUCK ANYMORE
BECAUSE BETRAYAL
ISN'T SURPRISING

I'D RATHER BE STABBED FROM THE FRONT
AT LEAST YOU'LL GIVE ME THE CHANCE
TO EXPECT IT TO COME

LIKE ME

IF YOU CAN'T LOOK ME IN THE EYES
I QUESTION WHO YOU REALLY ARE
ARE YOU GENUINE?
CAN I TRUST YOU?

OR MAYBE YOU'RE LIKE ME
YOU'RE HURTING INSIDE
AND YOU DON'T WANT ANYONE
TO FIGURE YOU OUT

UGLY

DON'T STARE AT ME
FOR TOO LONG
OR YOU'LL FIGURE OUT
I'M UGLY ON THE OUTSIDE
AND INSIDE

MATTER

I CARE TOO MUCH
ABOUT WHAT PEOPLE THINK OF ME
I LIKE TO STAY RESERVED
TO HIDE WHO I REALLY AM
BECAUSE I'M AFRAID PEOPLE WON'T LIKE WHO I AM
I *KNOW* PEOPLE WON'T LIKE WHO I AM

THE THING IS
I TRY TO PLEASE EVERYONE
EVEN THE ONES WHO DON'T LIKE ME

THOSE WHO MIND DON'T MATTER
AND THOSE WHO MATTER DON'T MIND
OR THAT'S WHAT THEY SAY
BUT TO ME
EVERYONE MATTERS
AND EVERYONE MINDS

HIDE

I TRY TO BE BRAVE
BUT I GET THIS FEELING IN MY HEART
TWISTING AND TURNING

I KNOW THE PAIN ALL TOO WELL
SO I TAKE THAT AS A WARNING

EXPLODE

I BOTTLE UP MY EMOTIONS AND FEELINGS
BECAUSE THERE IS NOTHING
FOR ME TO DO WITH THEM
I FEEL AS IF
MY HEART AND BRAIN
ARE ABOUT TO EXPLODE

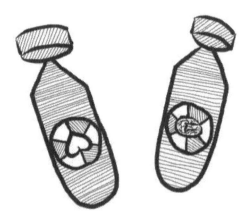

KARMA

I DON'T BELIEVE IN KARMA
TO HAVE BAD THINGS HAPPEN
ALL THROUGHOUT MY LIFE

FEELING WORSE AND WORSE
WHAT HAVE I DONE
TO DESERVE ALL THIS

MAYBE I'M JUST TOO FOCUSED
ON THE NEGATIVE
I DON'T REALIZE ALL THE POSITIVE

BUT I ALWAYS WRITE DOWN THE GOOD
BECAUSE THEY'RE BECOMING SO RARE
I'M AFRAID I'LL FORGET
WHAT *GOOD* FEELS LIKE

CHOICE

I DON'T CHOOSE
WHEN TO BE SAD
AND WHEN NOT TO BE
I JUST AM

AND IT'S NOT AS SIMPLE
AS JUST GETTING OVER IT
THESE FEELINGS ARE NOT EASY
TO OVERCOME

VULNERABLE

IT ISN'T AS EASY

OR AS SIMPLE

TO JUST OPEN YOURSELF UP TO SOMEONE

AND TALK ABOUT IT

THE FEELING OF VULNERABILITY

IS LIKE A GUN TO MY HEAD

I DON'T KNOW IF THE PERSON AIMING

HAS THE INTENTION OF DRIVING AWAY MY EVIL THOUGHTS

OR DRIVING A BULLET THROUGH MY BRAIN

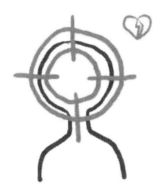

OPEN UP

I'M NOT SAD
SADNESS IS SOMETHING
THAT GOES AWAY
WHAT I HAVE
DOESN'T GO AWAY
IT ALWAYS COMES BACK
TO HAUNT ME

BAND-AID

TALKING ABOUT MY PROBLEMS
MAY HELP A LITTLE
BUT YOU CAN'T EXPECT A BAND-AID
TO HEAL A STAB WOUND

ONE OF THOSE

I KEEP THIS PROBLEM TO MYSELF
BECAUSE THERE'S THIS NEGATIVE STIGMA

I'M AFRAID TO SHARE IT
AND BEING KNOWN AS ONE OF THOSE

SELF-CENTERED

IT'S THAT FEELING OF
WANTING TO CRAWL BACK INSIDE
EVERYONE'S STARING
LABELLING, COMPARTMENTALIZING YOU

EW LOOK AT HIM
HE'S SO SKINNY, IS HE ANOREXIC?
DOES HE EVEN EAT?
IS HE GAY? AT LEAST BI
DOES HE EVEN KNOW ANYTHING?
HE DOESN'T SEEM TO BE SMART

BUT YOU WANT TO GO OUTSIDE
THOUGH YOUR SELF-ESTEEM CORRODED
BY PEOPLES UNNECESSARY CURIOSITY
DRAGS YOU DEEPER IN THE POISON

SELF-AWARE

ALL I EVER SEE
ARE MY FLAWS

MAGIC

MY EYES ALSO SEE
THE PAIN YOU'RE IN
FROM ALL MY EYES
HAVE SEEN TO DATE
NO MATTER WHAT FACE
YOU CHOOSE TO WEAR TODAY
KIND OF STRANGE I KNOW
IT'S LIKE I CAN FEEL YOUR PAIN

I'M TIRED

IT SEEMED TO BE A NATURAL DISTASTE
THAT I LEFT WITH PEOPLE
AS THEY FELT THE NEED TO ALWAYS LET ME KNOW
EVERY SINGLE THING ABOUT ME
THAT MADE ME DIFFERENT

WHILE IT TOOK BITS AND PIECES AWAY
LEAVING MY HEART DESOLATE
YET MY BRAIN IN A DAZE
FROM THE NUMEROUS TRAITS IT'S TRYING TO REPIECE
IN ORDER TO FIGURE OUT WHO I REALLY AM

ALL THIS
WEIGHS ON MY BODY
DRAGGING ME FURTHER IN
AND FURTHER DEEPER
I JUST WANT IT ALL TO END

VOID

I'M LOOKING
FOR SOMETHING
TO FILL THIS VOID
LEFT INSIDE ME

UNSATISFIED

EVEN I DON'T KNOW
IF THIS THING I'M LOOKING FOR
CAN EVER BE FOUND

BUT EVEN IF IT IS
I DON'T KNOW IF IT'S ENOUGH
TO SATE THE HUNGER

JUST RUN AWAY
BECAUSE I'M AFRAID
YOU'LL BE CONSUMED TOO

<u>GENUINE</u>

I VALUE BEING GENUINE
BUT I CAN'T EVEN BE GENUINE WITH MYSELF
WHAT A JOKE

<u>I DESERVE IT</u>

I ALWAYS TELL MYSELF
I DON'T DESERVE THE BAD THINGS
THAT HAPPENED TO ME
BUT IT'S COMING TO THE POINT
WHERE I DON'T KNOW
IF I'M SAYING THAT
BECAUSE I TRULY BELIEVE IT
OR IF I'M JUST LYING TO MYSELF

I CAN'T REMEMBER

THOSE COOL SUMMER NIGHTS
WHEN YOU LAY IN BED
THERE'S A LIGHT COOL BREEZE
COMING IN FROM THE WINDOW
THE SOFT MOONLIGHT
FLOWING THROUGH THE CURTAINS
AND YOU CAN HEAR THE CRICKETS CHIRPING
LAYING THERE WITH AN EMPTY MIND
NOTHING TO WORRY ABOUT

TELL ME
WHAT DOES THAT FEEL LIKE?

OK PT. I

NO MATTER HOW TOUGH
THINGS BECOME
I ALWAYS TELL MYSELF
IT'S GOING TO BE OK –
YOU'RE GOING TO BE OK
BECAUSE NO ONE ELSE WILL

OK PT. II

I'M STILL WAITING
FOR SOMEONE
TO TELL ME
THAT IT'S GOING TO BE OK

RUN

I FEEL LIKE EVERYTHING I'VE BEEN THROUGH TO THIS POINT
EVERYTHING I'VE EXPERIENCED THAT HAS BROUGHT ME HERE
HAS KEPT ME CHAINED DOWN INTO THE GROUND
PREVENTING ME FROM RUNNING AWAY AND LEAVING IT ALL
BEHIND

I KNEW THAT PEOPLE WOULDN'T BE ABLE TO HANDLE MY TRUTH
AS THROUGHOUT MY LIFE, I'VE BEEN GIVEN MANY SIGNALS
SOME OF COURSE, HAS BEEN MUCH MORE DIRECT THAN OTHERS
THAT WHAT I WAS OR MORE SPECIFICALLY, WHO I WAS, WAS A
PROBLEM

BUT I WAS ALREADY SO EMOTIONALLY AND MENTALLY CRIPPLED
I JUST COULDN'T DO IT - I WAS SCARED THAT I WOULDN'T BE
ABLE TO SURVIVE
AND THAT I WOULD FINALLY PROVE TO EVERYONE AND MYSELF
THAT I WAS IN FACT A COMPLETE WASTE OF A HUMAN

DARK SIDE OF THE MOON

THEY SAY THE MOON ONLY EVER
SHOWS ONE SIDE OF ITS FACE
MAYBE THE MOON'S AFRAID
OF SHOWING US ITS OTHER SIDE
ITS TRUE SIDE
OR MAYBE ITS ALL THAT FORCE
AND PULLING WE DO
THAT THE MOON CAN ONLY SHOW ONE SIDE
BUT DESPITE WHAT SIDE IT SHOWS US
IT'LL ALWAYS BE THE SAME
ON THE INSIDE

<u>END IT</u>

I JUST WANT IT TO END
I JUST WANT IT TO END
I JUST WANT IT TO END
I JUST WANT IT TO END
I JUST WANT IT TO END
I JUST WANT IT TO END
THEN END IT

ROSE

LIKE A ROSE

ITS SMELL

EVER SO CAPTIVATING

BUT THE CLOSER YOU GET

THE MORE THE THORNS WILL HURT

AND ONE DAY

YOU'LL UNDERSTAND

ALL THE THORNS

LEFT PIERCED IN MY LIFE

BLOOM

LIKE A FLOWER
I TAKE TIME TO GROW
AND ONCE IT'S FULLY BLOOMED
YOU WILL SEE ITS TRUE BEAUTY

BUT NOT ALL FLOWERS BLOOM
IT TAKES CARE AND PATIENCE
OR IT'LL JUST WILT
AND DIE

UNHAPPY

YOU KNOW YOU'RE UGLY
NOBODY LIKES YOU
YOU DESERVE NOTHING

- MY BRAIN

OBLIVIOUS

YOU SAY YOU'RE DOING EVERYTHING YOU CAN
FOR ME
DO YOU REALLY THINK
I'M THAT OBLIVIOUS TO YOUR LIES
YOU REALLY MUST THINK I'M A FOOL

FAKE

I FALL BACKWARDS

WITH MY HAND REACHING OUT

I SEE YOU STARING AT ME

AND JUST AS I CLOSE MY EYES

I CAN FEEL THE TIPS OF YOUR FINGERS

I OPEN MY EYES

BUT YOU PULL YOUR HAND BACK

YOU ONLY DID THAT

TO SAVE FACE

<u>KNOW</u>

DESPITE NOT KNOWING
MUCH ABOUT WHO I AM
FOR SOME REASON
OTHERS SEEM TO KNOW

RELATIONSHIP

TO ME
OUR RELATIONSHIP IS LIKE
HOLDING ONTO THE BLADE
OF A SWORD
THE HARDER I TRY AND HOLD ON
THE MORE IT HURTS

SMILE

SMILING DOESN'T ONLY MEAN
I'M HAPPY
IT TAKES ALL MY STRENGTH
AND WILL POWER

I'M TRYING TO FORGET

UNDERSTAND ME

WHAT HURTS ME
IS NOT THAT PEOPLE DON'T LIKE ME
IT'S THAT THEY REFUSE TO UNDERSTAND ME

DRAG ME TO HELL

I CAN FEEL WARM HANDS
WRAPPED AROUND MY NECK
TEARS FLOWING DOWN MY FACE
AS I LET MY FINAL BREATH ESCAPE
I'M AT EASE
KNOWING THIS IS FINALLY THE END
TO THE SUFFERING
AS I'M BEING DRAGGED
DOWN TO HELL

START OVER

IF YOU'RE UNHAPPY
THEN WHY DON'T YOU JUST LEAVE

BECAUSE I'M SCARED
OF STARTING OVER
AGAIN

FALLING DEEP

YOU
WERE SOMETHING SHINY
SOMETHING I WANTED

BUT I FELL HARD
AND DEEP
INTO YOUR EYES

WHICH ONLY ENDED UP
HURTING ME
BECAUSE ONLY FOOLS
WOULD FALL FOR YOU

KILL

IF I COULD KILL
I WOULDN'T FEEL A THING
MAYBE A LITTLE
FOR THE PARENTS
HAVING LOST SOMEONE THEY LOVED
WHY?
MINE LOST SOMEONE AS WELL
THEY JUST LOST THEIR ONLY SON

FUTURE

I'M SCARED TO SEE
WHAT THE FUTURE HOLDS
BECAUSE I DON'T THINK
YOU'RE THERE WITH ME

LOCKED OUT

I CAN'T OPEN MYSELF UP
I'VE ALREADY LOCKED MYSELF OUT
AND THROWN AWAY THE KEY

I HOPE
SOMEONE CAUGHT IT

BAGGAGE

IT'S THE THINGS THAT WERE SAID
AND THE THINGS THAT WERE DONE TO ME
I HAD TO ENDURE EVER SINCE I WAS YOUNG
EXPERIENCING LOST HOPE
BEFORE I EVEN KNEW OF ITS EXISTANCE
FABRICATED THIS ILLUSIONARY CAGE
THAT OPPRESSED MY SENSE OF SELF

I COULD BE SURROUNDED BY FAMILY OR FRIENDS
OR I CAN BE ALONE, LOST IN MY OWN THOUGHTS
DOESN'T MATTER IF I'M HAPPY, SAD OR ANYTHING INBETWEEN
I'M ALWAYS CARRYING THIS WEIGHT ON MY MIND

I PRESUME THERE'S THIS HUMANISTIC INCLINATION
TO BUILD CONNECTIONS WITH OTHERS
AS A WAY TO ENHANCE OUR LIVES
BUT NO ONE DESERVES THE BAGGAGE I HAVE –
WEIGHING ME DOWN
SO I END UP KEEPING TO MYSELF

SUN

THE SUN RISES WITHOUT FAIL
BUT I CAN'T ALWAYS SEE IT THAT WAY
IT SIGNALLED THE START
OF ANOTHER DAY
WHERE I'D DIE, JUST A LITTLE
EACH AND EVERYDAY
IT ROSE

SCARS

SOMETIMES
YOU MIGHT CATCH A GLIMPSE
OF THE PAIN I'M IN
IT'S WRITTEN ALL OVER MY BODY
IF YOU LOOK A LITTLE MORE CLOSELY
YOU'LL NOTICE MY SCARS ARE STILL OPEN
IT'S EASY TO CONCEAL ONE OR TWO
BUT I HAVE TOO MANY
TO KEEP THEM ALL HIDDEN

HARD TO LOVE

WHAT DOES IT MEAN TO LOVE
TO FEEL LOVED
THAT FEELING
IT'S SOMETHING
I CAN'T SEEM TO UNDERSTAND

.

WORTHY

I HATE RELATIONSHIPS
PRETENDING I'M NOT INTERESTED
BUT I THINK THE TRUTH IS
I'M NOT WORTHY OF ANYONES LOVE

I HATE EVERYTHING ABOUT ME
AND I THINK EVERYONE ELSE WILL TOO

I'M A HEAVY BURDEN TO BEAR
THAT'LL PROBABLY SCARE PEOPLE AWAY
I THINK MAYBE –
I'M JUST NOT WORTHY OF MYSELF

THANKS, I HOPE

IT TAKES A LOT OF COURAGE
TO OPEN UP
AND TO BE VULNERABLE
I'M TRYING

AND TO YOU
WHO WAS THERE
TO LISTEN
IT'S BECAUSE I TRUST(ED) YOU

CYCLING FEELINGS

PAINFUL EXPERIENCES
HAVE LEFT ME HOSTILE AND LONELY
THE LONELINESS EATS AWAY AT ME
EVEN THOUGH A CONNECTION
AND THE FEELING OF LOVE IS SOMETHING I CRAVE
BUT I FEAR OTHERS
ONLY BECAUSE I'M TRYING TO PROTECT MYSELF
FROM BEING HURT AGAIN
IT'S A VICIOUS CYCLE

SHARE

DO YOU HAVE
ENOUGH LOVE FOR ME
BECAUSE I DON'T
HAVE ENOUGH
TO LOVE MYSELF

STUCK INBETWEEN

IT'S ALWAYS THIS FEELING
THAT LINGERS
TELLING ME TO CROSS THE LINE
BUT I KNOW I SHOULDN'T
BECAUSE ONCE I CROSS
THERE *IS* NO TURNING BACK

HOPE

I THINK WE'RE ALL BORN WITH SOME SORT OF LIGHT INSIDE OF US/ENTERING THE WORLD WITH OUR EYES WIDE/SEEMINGLY FULL OF LIFE, HAPPINESS, HOPE/ALL THESE THINGS BEFORE WE COULD EVEN GRASP WHAT THEY WERE/WE LAUGHED AND WE CRIED BUT NOTHING WE COULDN'T RECOVER FROM

THEN ALL OF A SUDDEN, YOUR EYES OPEN TO A NEW WORLD/THIS ONE LOOKS THE EXACT SAME BUT THERE'S SOMETHING DIFFERENT/THERE ARE PEOPLE JUST LIKE YOU, OR SO YOU THOUGHT/THEY WERE BORN THE SAME WAY YOU WERE/ENTERING THE WORLD WITH THEIR EYES WIDE OPEN/FULL OF LIFE, HAPPINESS, HOPE/MAYBE THEIR JOURNEY TO THIS POINT IN LIFE WAS DIFFERENT/BUT THERE'S NO WAY YOU WOULD'VE KNOWN THAT/YOU WERE ONLY 9, MAYBE 10?

IT SEEMED LIKE THEY HAD THIS URGE TO DIM YOUR LIGHT/THEY WANTED YOUR FIRE TO GO OUT/YOU NEVER KNEW WHY/YOU DIDN'T HAVE ANYTHING THEY WOULD WANT/AND EVEN THOUGH YOU HAD NOTHING TO OFFER, THEY CONTINUED/THEY PICKED YOU APART/AND EVEN WHEN YOU WERE STILL TRYING TO RECOVER THE MISSING PIECES/THEY MADE IT HARDER FOR YOU/MAYBE WITH A KICK, MAYBE A JAB — YOU COULD NEVER FULLY RECOVER/THEY WANTED YOU GONE, THEY WANTED YOU DEAD/ AND GUESS WHAT? I ALSO WANTED TO BE DEAD/I WANTED IT ALL TO STOP/I WANTED THE PAIN INSIDE THAT KEPT ME UP AT NIGHT TO STOP/I WANTED THE FEAR OF FACING IT ALL OVER AGAIN THE NEXT DAY TO STOP THE LIGHT INSIDE WAS ABOUT TO GO OUT/BUT EVEN THE TINEST AMOUNT OF LIGHT EMITS A SENSE OF HOPE/AND HONESTLY, NOW THAT I'M IN MY 20'S/I DON'T KNOW WHAT IT WAS EXACTLY, THAT KEPT MY CANDLE LIT/MAYBE FOR THIS VERY REASON — WHAT YOU'RE READING RIGHT NOW/I GUESS YOU EITHER FIND THAT SPARK OR IGNITE IT YOURSELF/GLAD, I'M STILL HERE

<u>I GIVE UP</u>

I WANT TO BE STRONG
I WANT TO BE HAPPY
I WANT TO BE COURAGEOUS
BUT GIVING UP
BECOMES EASIER

PAINFUL

LIVING
IS THE MOST PAINFUL

GROWTH

WE GROW
FROM OUR EXPERIENCES
PAIN HURTS THE MOST
WHEN YOU FIRST EXPERIENCE IT
BUT AFTER THE SECOND, THIRD
FOURTH TIME...
IT HURTS LESS AND LESS
MAYBE WE'VE GROWN STRONGER
OR MAYBE I'M JUST SO USED TO GETTING HURT
I'VE BECOME NUMB TO THE PAIN

WATCH OUT

WE HAVE TO
WATCH OUT FOR OURSELVES
BECAUSE NO ONE ELSE WILL

YOU CAN TRUST SOMEONE
BUT THEY'LL END UP
STABBING YOU IN THE BACK

HERE

MAYBE
IF YOU
GRABBED MY HAND
AS I WAS FALLING
I WOULD STILL BE HERE
WITH YOU

MAYBE
IF YOU
TURNED AROUND
AS I WAS CRYING OUT FOR YOU
I WOULD STILL BE HERE
WITH YOU

MAYBE
IF YOU
KEPT MY LOVE
MY TRUST
SAFE WITH YOU
I WOULD STILL BE HERE
WITH YOU

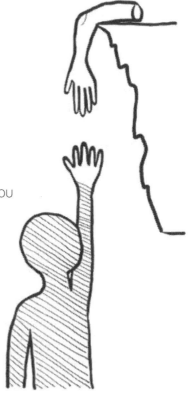

NEVER LET GO

IT'S NOT ABOUT BEING HAPPY
OR SIMPLY LEARNING TO BE HAPPY AGAIN
IT'S ABOUT SUFFERING
AND CONTINUING TO SUFFER

NEVER LETTING GO OF THE PAST
BUT STILL LIVING ON

BECAUSE THOSE MEMORIES
THOSE EXPERIENCES
HAVE EATEN A PART OF YOU
TO LET THEM GO
MEANS LOSING PIECES OF YOURSELF

HAPPY MASK

YOUR SMILE IS LIKE AN ILLUSION
A TRICK ONLY USED TO DIVERT
KEEPING PEOPLE FROM DISCOVERING
YOUR BROKEN HEART AND BROKEN BONES
HOW YOUR MIND HAS BEEN CLOUDED
BY YOUR THOUGHTS OF PAST TRAUMA

SOMETHING I GENUINELY ENVY
WHAT I REALIZE AS TRUE STRENGTH
TO CONTINUALLY PUT THAT SMILE
ON YOUR FACE
EVERYDAY
DESPITE YOUR SUFFERING

PIERCER

I'M TRYING TO HEAL MY WOUNDS
BUT I DON'T THINK I CAN DO IT ALONE
I CAN'T PICK UP PIECES
OF MY HEART WHEN IT SHATTERED
INTO A MILLION TINY FRAGMENTS
IT WAS FRAGILE – MADE OF GLASS
BUT DESPITE THE TITANIUM EXTERIOR
I HAD BUILT
SOMETHING ALWAYS FINDS ITS WAY
INSIDE

<u>CATCH ME</u>

CAN YOU BE THERE
TO CATCH ME
AS I FALL?

WHAT IS REALITY

IT'S COMING
TO THAT POINT
WHERE I CAN NO LONGER
DISTINGUISH BETWEEN
MY NIGHTMARES
AND MY REALITY
THEY'RE BECOMING ONE IN THE SAME

DOES REALITY EQUAL TRUTH

WHAT EVEN IS REALITY?
THE PERSON OUR PARENTS TAUGHT US TO BE?
THE CHARACTER TRAITS OUR AQUANTINCES, TEACHERS, FRIENDS,
BULLIES, AND STRANGERS LABELLED US?
THE OVERMASCULIZATION OF MEN ON TV?
OR MAYBE THE DEMASCULIZATION OF CERTAIN ACTIONS,
STATURES, RACES, AND DIFFERENT *TYPES* OF MEN?

HOW I FEEL ABOUT MYSELF
ARE BASED ON THESE REALITIES
SO, CAN THEY BE CONSIDERED REALITY?
CAN THEY BE CONSIDERED THE TRUTH?

BORN TO SUFFER

WE SUFFER BECAUSE OF LOVE
AND WE SUFFER WITHOUT LOVE
WE SUFFER BECAUSE WE ARE ALONE
AND WE SUFFER BECAUSE OF THE PEOPLE AROUND US

DOES LIVING MEAN TO SUFFER?
OR DOES SUFFERING MEAN WE'RE LIVING?
MAYBE BOTH CAN ONLY EXIST WITH THE OTHER

TEARS

EACH TEAR
DOWN MY FACE
IS A SCAR
LEFT IN MY HEART

I MISS

I MISS THE REALITY I ONCE HAD
LAUGHING AND SMILING UNTROUBLED
WITHOUT MY HEART STUCK IN MELANCHOLY

I MISS THE SANITY I ONCE HAD
WHEN MY MIND SEEKED SALVATION
PROVIDING CLARITY FROM THE MENTAL OVERLOAD

I MISS THE INNOCENCE I ONCE HAD
UNASSUMING OF PEOPLE THAT SURROUNDED ME
THE EASE OF MIND THAT THE LUXURIES OF NAIVETY PROVIDED

PLEASE LIKE ME

I TRIED BEING MYSELF
BUT NO ONE LIKED THAT
I TRIED BEING SOMEONE ELSE
HOPING I WOULD FIT IN
BUT THAT DIDN'T WORK EITHER
I WANTED TO BELONG
SO BAD
BUT NOTHING I DID WORKED
I KEPT GETTING HURT
SO I CLOSED MYSELF OFF
TO PROTECT MY HEART
BECAUSE NO ONE ELSE WOULD
NOW I HAVE NO IDEA WHO I AM
NOR DO I WANT TO BE SOMEONE ELSE

<u>LEAVE ME ALONE</u>

I WISH THEY WOULD'VE
JUST LEFT ME ALONE
I DIDN'T NEED TO BE ACKNOWLEDGED
I DIDN'T WANT ANYTHING FROM THEM
BUT THEY FELT THE NEED TO SAY SOMETHING
THEY NEEDED TO TAKE SOMETHING FROM ME
AND ALL I COULD THINK WAS
WHY ME?
JUST
LEAVE ME ALONE
PLEASE

TOUCH

THAT MOMENT
YOU TOUCHED ME
WILL NEVER DISAPPEAR
FROM MY MEMORIES
I WAS YOUNG AND AFRAID
AND YOU TOOK ADVANTAGE
OF ME
AND THE SITUATION I WAS IN
ALONE
VULNERABLE

HELP ME

THOSE WERE THE TIMES WHEN I WOULD JUST WAKE UP
EYES HALF OPEN, FOLLOWING THE SAME BRAINLESS ROUTINE
THE ONLY THING I COULD EVER STOMACH
WAS A BOWL OF FLEETING HOPE
AND A DOSE OF I DON'T GIVE A FUCK
BECAUSE I KNEW OF THIS NEVER-ENDING CYCLE
I HAD BEEN CONDEMNED TO

SOMEDAYS I WOULD FIGHT BACK
BUT MOST DAYS, I NEVER HAD THE ENERGY
THE PAIN HAD ALREADY ERODED MY SENSE OF SELF
SO I STOOD THERE, TAKING EVERYTHING THROWN AT ME

EVEN THOUGH I TRIED MY HARDEST TO NEVER SHOW WEAKNESS
TO THE EYES OF THOSE WHO HURT ME
THE DAY WOULD END WITH MY FEET DRAGGING THE REST OF MY
BODY HOME
CRASHING FACE FIRST ONTO MY BED
HEAD FULL OF THOUGHTS AND EYES FULL OF TEARS
I NEVER KNEW, HOW MUCH MORE OF THIS I COULD HANDLE

<u>I NEED YOU</u>

I NEEDED YOU
TO BE THERE FOR ME
BUT YOU
WERE JUST STANDING
IN THE SIDELINES
WATCHING ME EAT SHIT
AND THEN LEFT

ARGUE

THE ONLY THING
I CAN REMEMBER
FROM MY CHILDHOOD
WERE THE ARGUMENTS

THEY WENT ON AND ON
EVEN TIL THIS DAY
IS THIS WHAT LOVE IS?
BECAUSE I DON'T WANT ANY OF IT

FAMILY VALUES

IN THIS FAMILY
MONEY IS EVERYTHING
YOU CAN BUY ANYTHING
EVEN HAPPINESS

BUT GREED
IS RUINING THIS FAMILY
THE END IS COMING
IT'S ONLY A MATTER OF TIME

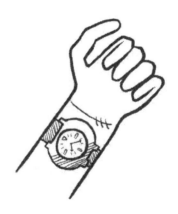

BLOODLINE

YOU HAVE TO KNOW
THAT THERE'S SOMETHING
DIFFERENT ABOUT ME
RIGHT?

I DON'T KNOW
IF YOU'LL SUPPORT ME FULLY
AND I'M AFRAID
BECAUSE YOU'RE THE REMAINING THREAD
THAT KEEPS ME CONNECTED
TO THE REST OF OUR BLOODLINE

SO I'M AFRAID
TO REVEAL THE TRUTH
MY TRUTH

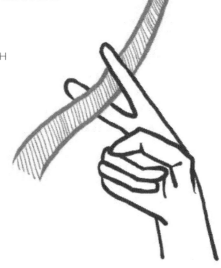

SIBLING

THIS BURDEN
IS MINE TO BEAR
AND SHOULD BE MINE ALONE
BUT UNFORTUNATELY
IT'LL BLEED INTO YOUR LIFE

I DON'T KNOW
IF I'LL STILL BE HERE
TO BE YOUR BROTHER -
A PART OF THE FAMILY

AND TO HELP SUPPORT
FINANCIALLY
EMOTIONALLY
ONLY TIME WILL TELL

I'M SORRY

FAMILY

I DIDN'T WANT TO BELIEVE
THAT THIS FAMILY
WOULDN'T SURVIVE

TOO MANY SECRETS AND LIES
THE SCENT OF MONEY
CAUSES A FRENZY

THERE'S NO LOVE
SQUINT AND IT BECOMES CLEAR
THE DISCONNECT

WE'RE BORN INTO OUR FAMILIES
IT WAS NEVER A CHOICE
THE CHOICE IS
IF YOU WANT TO CONTINUE SUFFERING
OR NOT

IT'S HARD TO ACCEPT THE FACT
THAT WE COULDN'T BE
LIKE OTHER LOVING FAMILIES

THE PATH ENCOURAGED

I CHOSE MY PATH
BECAUSE I WAS TAUGHT THAT
MONEY MEANS YOU'LL BE SAFE
MONEY MEANS YOU'LL BE HAPPY
MONEY MEANS YOU'LL LIVE AN EASY LIFE

AND THROUGH THAT JOURNEY
THEY NEVER WARNED ME THAT
I WOULD FEEL SO LOST
I WOULD FEEL SO UNMOTIVATED
I WOULD FEEL SO EMPTY INSIDE

WHEN YOU AIMLESSLY FOLLOW THE PATH
CARVED OUT FOR YOU
YOU'LL ALWAYS END UP LOST
I FINALLY REALIZED THAT BUT I WAS ALREADY TOO LATE
I STILL FEEL AS LOST AS EVER

FADE INTO DARKNESS

DARKNESS ONLY COMES
WHEN EVERYTHING ELSE IS GONE
THE DIMMING LIGHT
INSIDE OF ME
THAT I HAVE STRUGGLED
TO KEEP ALIVE
IS ABOUT TO BE OVERTAKEN

I HOPE YOU CARED

HUG ME
AND HOLD ME TIGHT
JUST FOR A LITTLE
WHILE YOU STAB ME
IN THE BACK
SO I AT LEAST KNOW
YOU CARED ABOUT ME ONCE
AND THAT I WASN'T
A COMPLETE FOOL

PROBLEMS

DWELLING ON OUR PROBLEMS
MAKES US MISERABLE
IGNORING OUR PROBLEMS
CAUSES US TO BECOME MISERABLE

SOLUTIONS
AREN'T EASILY FOUND
I'VE SEARCHED TO THE BACK OF MY BRAIN
BUT ALL I CAN FIND EVER IS PAIN

I CAN'T KEEP IGNORING THEM
BECAUSE MORE APPEAR
MAKING A HOME FOR THEMSELVES
IN THE CREVICES OF MY BRAIN

IT'S TAKING A TOLL
WEIGHING MY HEART DOWN
THOUGH I CAN'T TRUST ANYONE
TO HELP

LOOK AT YOURSELF

WHEN YOU HAVE TO
LOOK IN THE MIRROR
AND TELL YOURSELF
TO SMILE
TELL YOURSELF
TO BE HAPPY
YOU'RE ONLY GOING TO SUFFER

<u>5</u>

I LOVED
YOU. LEFT
ME BY MYSELF

REPRESS

WHY AM I ENCOURAGED
TO REPRESS MY EMOTIONS
I SHOULDN'T BE SAD
BECAUSE THAT MAKES YOU LOOK UNFRIENDLY
I SHOULDN'T CRY
BECAUSE THAT MAKES YOU LOOK WEAK
I'M ONLY HUMAN
AND HUMANS HAVE EMOTIONS

I'M SCARED

THE SIGNS ARE SUBTLE
BUT ONCE YOU MISS THEM
IT'S OVER
AND I'LL BE GONE

IT'S TOO LATE

THEY SEEMED HAPPY
BUT THAT'S WHAT EVERYONE SAYS
AFTER IT'S TOO LATE

I'M HURT

MY HEART
ISN'T MADE OF GLASS
BUT IT SHATTERED

MY BODY
ISN'T SURROUNDED BY WATER
BUT IT'S DROWNING

MY FACE
HAS A SMILE
BUT MY HEART
STILL ACHES

<u>I DECIDE MY FATE</u>

LUCK IS NEVER
SOMETHING I BELIEVED IN
YOU GET WHAT YOU DESERVE
AND I DON'T DEPEND ON LUCK
TO DETERMINE MY FATE
I DECIDE THAT
FOR MYSELF
BUT I GUESS FATE
MIGHT HAVE LED ME TO THE END

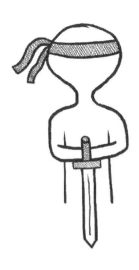

I AM HAPPY THOUGH, AT TIMES

THERE ARE NUMEROUS TIMES
WHERE I'M GENUINELY HAPPY
BUT THAT DOESN'T MEAN
MY NEGATIVE EXPERIENCES
JUST DISAPPEAR
THEY CLOUD MY THOUGHTS

CLOSING MY EYES
JUST LONGER THAN A BLINK
THOSE MOMENTS BURNED
IN THE BACK OF MY EYELIDS
MY BRAIN WILL NEVER FORGET
TO REMIND ME OF THOSE TIMES

JUST BE HAPPY

I WANT YOU TO UNDERSTAND
THAT I CAN'T *JUST BE HAPPY*
IGNORING ALL THOSE EXPERIENCES
BECAUSE THEY WERE THE ONES
THAT DESTROYED ME
BROKE ME
LEFT THORNS IN MY HEART
AND THOUGH I CAN'T FORGET
THE HOLES THEY'VE LEFT
I TRY EXTREMELY HARD
TO CONTINUE LIVING
AND TRY TO BE HAPPY DESPITE THEM
BUT THE PAIN OF THE THORNS
WILL ALWAYS REMAIN

WE NEED HELP, I NEED HELP

MENTAL HEALTH
SHOULDN'T BE SOMETHING
WE'RE AFRAID TO TALK ABOUT
BUT IT'S UNFORTUNATE
WE HAVE TO KEEP QUIET
BECAUSE OF THE STIGMA

I'M NOT LESS OF
A FRIEND
A LOVE
A PERSON
BECAUSE OF IT

BUT MY MENTAL HEALTH
ISN'T SOMETHING THAT
CAN BE CURED ON ITS OWN
BY IGNORING IT
WE CAN'T DO EVERYTHING ALONE

GOODBYE

IT'S HARD TO CHASE
SOMETHING THAT'S ALREADY GONE

JUST RUN AWAY FROM ME
BECAUSE ALMOST EVERYONE ELSE HAS

TAKE MY LIFE

WHY DO YOU FEEL
THE NEED TO TAKE
FROM SOMEONE
WHO HAS NOTHING?

I DON'T HAVE THE BRAINS
THAT YOU HAVE
I DON'T HAVE THE SET DIRECTION FOR MY LIFE
THAT YOU HAVE
I DON'T HAVE THE AMOUNT OF FRIENDS
THAT YOU HAVE
I DON'T HAVE THE LOVE
THAT YOU HAVE

I HAVE NOTHING
FOR YOU TO TAKE
WHAT DO YOU WANT FROM ME?
MY LIFE?

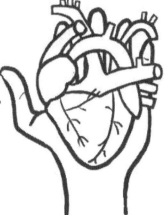

THE END

WHO KNEW
THAT THE ENDING OF MY STORY
BEGAN WHEN I FIRST MET YOU

DO YOU KNOW WHAT HAPPY IS

ARE YOU HAPPY?

WHAT DO YOU MEAN?
IN WHAT SENSE?

IN GENERAL. ARE YOU HAPPY
WITH WHERE YOU ARE IN LIFE?

I DON'T THINK I AM?
I'M NOT TOO SURE WHAT HAPPINESS IS
NOR DO I KNOW WHAT MAKES ME HAPPY

HIGH HOPES

I SET MY
HOPES TOO HIGH
THAT NO ONE
CAN EVER LIVE UP TO THEM
NOT EVEN ME

I'M TIRED PT. II

I HOPE PEOPLE CHANGE
BECAUSE I'M TIRED
OF BEING SOMEONE I'M NOT

PAINFUL WORDS

WHY AREN'T YOU SMARTER

WHY CAN'T YOU BE LIKE HIM

YOU LOOK LIKE A MONSTER

WHY ARE YOU EVEN HERE? YOU DON'T BELONG HERE

NO ONE COULD EVER LOVE YOU, YOU'RE BROKEN

GO KILL YOURSELF

MY WORLD IS CRUMBLING

MY LIFE IS THE WAY IT IS
BECAUSE OF THE CHOICES I'VE MADE
I WANTED TO LIVE HAPPY AND CAREFREE
I CHOSE TO BE MYSELF
BUT PEOPLE DIDN'T LIKE THAT
SO THEY HURT ME
AND ABUSED ME
I HAD NOTHING FOR THEM
I HAD NO ONE
I CHOSE TO BE STONE COLD AND EMOTIONLESS
AND THAT PUSHED PEOPLE AWAY FROM ME
I CLOSED MYSELF OFF
MY WORLD IS CRUMBLING
AND IT'S MY FAULT

HOW DO YOU KNOW

IT GETS BETTER
BUT HOW CAN YOU EVEN
SAY SOMETHING LIKE THAT
WHEN YOU HAVE NO IDEA
HOW I'M FEELING
OR WHAT I'VE BEEN THROUGH

THE ONLY THING
THAT GETS BETTER
IS YOUR CONSCIOUS
DO YOU REALLY THINK
IT'S MY FIRST TIME HEARING THAT

ALWAYS ALONE

IT'S THIS FEELING
THAT NO MATTER HOW MANY PEOPLE
ARE AROUND YOU
YOU STILL FEEL LONELY

UNCONTROLLABLE

IT'S THAT MOMENT
WHEN YOU REALIZE
YOU'RE IN THIS
BY YOURSELF
AND YOU CAN'T STOP
YOURSELF FROM CRYING

ADDICTED TO IT

IT'S LIKE THIS FEELING
OF SADNESS IS ADDICTING
THE PAIN IT BRINGS TO MY HEART
IS SOMETHING I'M SO USED TO NOW
IT'S COMFORTING
WHY ELSE
WOULD I *WANT* TO KEEP
COMING BACK TO THIS FEELING

SELF-WORTH

I MAY NOT REALIZE
MY OWN WORTH
BUT WHAT I DO KNOW
IS THAT YOU DON'T DESERVE ME

HEAL

SOME SCARS
NEVER FADE
SOME CUTS
NEVER HEAL

BLOOD-STAINED

YOUR SHIRT IS SOAKED
YOUR HANDS ARE COVERED
IT'S DRIPPING FROM YOUR FACE

YOU DUG YOUR HANDS
INTO MY CHEST
AND RIPPED OUT MY HEART

YOU THREW IT AWAY
AND YET YOU'RE BACK
WHAT ELSE DO YOU WANT FROM ME

DON'T FORGET ME

ONE DAY
YOU'LL FORGET ABOUT ME
BUT I'LL NEVER
FORGET ABOUT YOU

CARE

TELL ME YOU'LL TAKE CARE OF ME
AND I'LL DO THE SAME FOR YOU

YOU KNOW I KNOW

IT'S HARD FOR ME
TO TRUST PEOPLE
BUT TO KNOW THAT
YOU ACTUALLY CARE
MAKES ME HAPPY

BELIEVE

YOU KNOW
I BELIEVE YOU
RIGHT?
I TRUST YOU

1207

YOU NEVER REALLY EXPECT
OR AT LEAST, I NEVER EXPECTED
SOMEONE I NEVER REALLY KNEW
TO ACT THIS WAY
IT WAS DIFFERENT
I WAS HONESTLY SHOCKED
YOU REALLY CARED
AND YOU HAD MY BACK
EVEN THOUGH I TRIED TO HIDE EVERYTHING
I PRETENDED TO BE FINE
I TOLD YOU I WAS FINE
NOW, I GUESS I FEEL BAD FOR LYING TO YOU
I DIDN'T WANT TO DISAPPOINT YOU
BUT THANK YOU

OPPO PT. I

ALMOST NO ONE KNOWS WHAT I'M REALLY
LIKE. AND IT'S BECAUSE
I DON'T TRUST A LOT OF PEOPLE. BUT YOU
CAN PROBABLY TELL
I TRULY
APPRECIATE THAT YOU'VE ALWAYS BEEN THERE FOR ME

OPPO PT. II

SOMEDAY WE'LL ALL MOVE
ON AND LIVE OUR OWN LIVES. BUT I
HOPE THAT WE'LL STILL BE CLOSE.
YOU ARE
UNLIKE ANY OTHER PERSON I'VE MET. I WILL
NEVER FORGET WHAT WE'VE BEEN THROUGH, TOGETHER

CHOOSE

LIFE IS ALREADY HARD AS IT IS
THERE'S NO ADVANTAGE FOR ME
TO HAVE *CHOSE* TO LIVE THE LIFE I'M LIVING

WHY WOULD I *CHOOSE*
TO LIVE A MORE DIFFICULT LIFE
THAT'S BECAUSE
I DIDN'T CHOOSE

EASE

TIME CAN EASE THE PAIN
BUT I DON'T THINK
IT CAN HEAL MY HEART

GREY

I'M WALKING DOWN THIS GREY PATH

SEEMINGLY ENDLESS

WITH NOTHING IN SIGHT

I TURN AROUND

AND I SEE

THE SAME ENDLESS GREY PATH

FOLLOWING BEHIND ME

<u>INCOMPLETE</u>

I NO LONGER HAVE THE STRENGTH
TO PICK UP PIECES OF MYSELF
THAT YOU TOOK FROM ME

USED UNTIL IT WAS WORN AND BROKEN
THEN YOU DISCARDED THEM
AND LEFT ME INCOMPLETE

TRUST

THE THING IS
I DON'T NEED YOU
TO PROTECT ME
AND I DON'T NEED YOU
TO GO OUT OF YOUR WAY
TO SHOW THAT YOU'RE TRYING
I JUST NEED TO KNOW
THAT YOU DO
AND THAT I CAN
COMPLETELY
TRUST YOU

JUST THOUGHT YOU SHOULD KNOW

I DON'T NEED OR WANT
YOU TO FEEL SORRY FOR ME
NOR DO I NEED YOU TO FEEL
LIKE YOU HAVE TO GO THAT EXTRA MILE

I DIDN'T HAVE YOUR HELP
WHEN I HAD TO PULL MYSELF
OUT OF THE DARK ENDLESS HOLE
I WAS PUSHED INTO
AGAIN AND AGAIN

I WANTED TO SHARE MY STORY
WITH YOU
IT WAS BECAUSE I-
JUST THOUGHT YOU SHOULD KNOW

FOR GRANTED

ONCE YOU'RE LEFT EMPTY
SOMETHING HAS TO FILL THE SPACE
YOU LOOK FOR WORDS OF AFFIRMATION
TO STOW AWAY, HOPING IT OCCUPIES THE EMPTINESS
SO THAT IT DOESN'T CONTINUE BLEEDING
EVERYWHERE YOU GO

NOT ONLY IS MY HEART ON MY SLEEVE
BUT IT WAS GIVEN TO YOU, TRUSTING YOU
WHEN YOU WORE A MASK OF INNOCENCE
TO HIDE THE MONSTER INSIDE
ABLE TO CONCEAL YOUR TRUE INTENTIONS
EVEN WHEN DARKNESS LEAKED FROM THE CRACKS

I CAN'T HELP BUT BE STUCK
BEHIND THIS WALL OF DISAPPOINTMENT
THAT BUILT ITSELF OVER YEARS
WHEN EVERYONE HAS TAKEN MY HEART FOR GRANTED
THE EMPTINESS INSIDE SERVES AS A REMINDER, NONETHELESS
THAT EVIL EXISTS TO ROB US FROM OURSELVES

ANTICIPATION

SOMETIMES YOU'RE JUST TRYING TO LIVE LIFE
LIKE EVERYONE ELSE IS
BUT OUT OF NO WHERE, TO NO FAULT OF YOUR OWN
YOU'RE BOMBARDED WITH HATE
LEFT SO CONFUSED AND DEFEATED
BECAUSE IT WOULD BE DAY AFTER DAY
ANTICIPATING THE UNWARRANTED HATRED

THERE COMES A POINT
YOU STOP BEING HOPEFUL THAT IT'LL STOP
BECAUSE WHEN YOU TRIED ASKING FOR HELP
WHEN YOU CRIED OUT FOR HELP
NO ONE REALLY UNDERSTOOD YOU
MOST PEOPLE BLAMED YOU OR MADE THE SITUATION WORSE

YOU BEGAN TO ACCEPT
THAT NO ONE WOULD EVER UNDERSTAND
AND EVERY NIGHT WHEN YOU WENT TO BED
YOU'D HOPE TO WAKE UP FROM THIS NIGHTMARE
NOT THAT THESE WOULD BECOME
THE MEMORIES YOUR MIND WOULD REPLAY
EVERYTIME YOU THOUGHT OF YOUR PAST

SILENCE

SOMETIMES I JUST WANT TO CRAWL INTO A CORNER
SITTING WITH KNEES TO MY CHEST
ARMS WRAPPED ACROSS MY KNEES
EYES CLOSED IN COMPLETE SILENCE
JUST SO THAT I CAN JUST CLEAR MY MIND

SUN PT. II

ONE DAY
THE FIRE INSIDE WILL DIE
IT'S INEVITABLE
AND WE WILL COLLAPSE
INTO OURSELVES
AND START RAVAGING
ANYTHING AND EVERYTHING
THAT'S IN OUR PATH
UNCONTROLLABLY

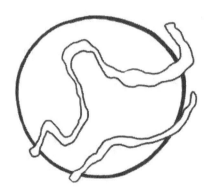

FOCUS

I FEEL THE PRESSURE IN MY EYES BUILD UP
AS IF THE CLOUDS COULDN'T HOLD ANYMORE TEARS
AND THE RAIN JUST STARTS FALLING

THOUGHTS, MEMORIES AND EXPERIENCES
BUZZING AROUND IN MY HEAD
LIKE AN ANGRY NEST OF BEES
AND I JUST CAN'T THINK STRAIGHT

I WANT TO CURL UP UNDER MY BLANKET
SUFFOCATING MY FACE UNDER THE PILLOW CRYING
BECAUSE IN THAT MOMENT
IT FEELS AS IF I WAS FLOATING ON WATER-
MY HEAD CLEAR AND I FINALLY GET TO FOCUS ON MYSELF

GROWING UP

I DIDN'T HAVE THE LUXURY
TO GROW UP AS MYSELF
I HAD TO GROW UP
BEING ANOTHER VERSION OF MYSELF
A COMPLETELY DIFFERENT PERSONA
I HAD TO PROTECT MY HEART
AND NOW AS I GROW OLDER
I HAVE TO FIGURE OUT
WHICH PARTS ARE ACTUALLY ME

DID YOU KNOW

DID YOU KNOW
WHEN YOU BROKE ME
I'M STILL PICKING UP THE PIECES

DID YOU KNOW
WHEN YOU CUT ME
BLOOD STILL SEEPS FROM THE SCARS

DID YOU KNOW
WHEN YOU PUSHED ME
I FELL TOO FAR TO CLIMB BACK

DID YOU KNOW
YOU FUCKED ME OVER

SEXUAL ORIENTATION

I ALWAYS WONDERED WHY
PEOPLE WERE SO CURIOUS
ABOUT MY SEXUAL ORIENTATION

DOES THAT DETERMINE
IF I'M GOING TO BE A GOOD PERSON
ABOVE HOW I TREAT OTHERS?

OF COURSE, IT'S A PART OF ME
BUT IT ISN'T NOR SHOULD IT BE
MY DEFINING CHARACTERISTIC

SOME DON'T CARE, SOME HAVE BEEN WAITING
DAYS, YEARS, MY WHOLE LIFETIME TO HEAR:
I AM... DIFFERENT

NEVER AGAIN

TOWERED OVER ME
OVERPOWERING ME
YOUR SHARP GAZE
AS IF IT SLIT MY THROAT
I WAS GASPING
AND I WAS STRUGGLING
FOR MY LIFE
AS YOU DID WHAT YOU WANTED

SOMETIMES I WAKE UP
WITH MY EYES STILL CLOSED
AND MY BODY FROZEN
BUT MY MIND RUNNING-
AWAY FROM YOU

AND NOT BECAUSE OF YOU
BUT BECAUSE OF THE STRENGTH I HAD-
STRUGGLED TO UNEARTH FROM WITHIN ME
I GREW AND I LEARNED
AND I WILL NEVER LET ANYONE
DO WHAT YOU DID TO ME
EVER AGAIN

TEMPORARY

YOU TELL ME THAT
PAIN IS ONLY TEMPORARY
AS IT ALWAYS SUBSIDES
BUT YOU CAN'T TELL ME
HOW LONG IT WILL LAST
1 MINUTE, 1 DAY, 1 YEAR, 1 LIFETIME?
AND NEITHER CAN I

DOMINO EFFECT

THE BROKEN ARE ALWAYS THE ONES BREAKING OTHERS

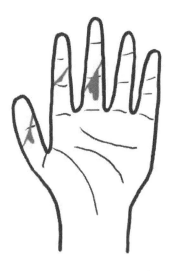

WHAT I WANTED

I SEE FAMILIES LAUGHING AND SMILING
ENJOYING EACH OTHERS COMPANY
AROUND THE DINNER TABLE
MAYBE THAT'S THE THING I WANTED ALL ALONG

I SEE COUPLES LAUGHING AND SMILING
CAPTIVATED BY EACH OTHERS LOVE
STROLLING DOWN THE STREET
MAYBE THAT'S THE THING I WANTED ALL ALONG

I SEE PEOPLE LAUGHING AND SMILING
CONFIDENT IN THEMSELVES
NOT CARING ABOUT WHAT OTHERS THINK
MAYBE THAT'S THE THING I WANTED ALL ALONG

YOU DON'T KNOW WHAT TO DO

SOMETIMES YOU'LL FEEL SO LOST
WITH YOUR MIND OVERCROWDED
YOUR HEART COMPLETELY EMPTY

YOUR EYES OPEN
AND ALL YOU SEE IS DARKNESS
YOUR EARS ALERT
BUT YOU DON'T HEAR A SOUND

NO DIRECTION AT ALL
YOU DON'T KNOW WHAT ELSE TO DO
BUT TO SIT THERE... LOST

LIFES A GAMBLE

REVEALING OUR TRUE SELVES
IS OUR GAMBLE ON LIFE
YOU RISK IT ALL
BEING YOURSELF
AND YOU EITHER WIN
OR YOU LOSE EVERYTHING
YOU ONCE HAD OR WERE

WHAT ACTUALLY MATTERS

IT DOESN'T MATTER
WHAT I AM
IT'S WHO I AM

LEARN

WHEN I WAS 10
I LEARNED THAT
I COULDN'T TRUST ANYONE

WHEN I WAS 16
I LEARNED THAT
I COULDN'T TRUST MY FAMILY

WHEN I WAS 21
I LEARNED THAT
TRUST NEVER EVEN EXISTED

GOAL

THE GOAL
WAS ALWAYS TO PROVE
PEOPLE WRONG

BUT THAT
ONLY MAKES YOU
VENGEFUL

THE GOAL
SHOULD HAVE BEEN
YOUR HAPPINESS

BARE

IT'S SCARY
BECAUSE THIS BOOK
IS MY HEART AND MY SOUL
MY MIND AND MY EYES

IT'S RAW AND PURE
THERE'S NOTHING
TO PROTECT ME
AS YOU READ ME

DROWN OUT

THE MUSIC TURNED
AS LOUD AS IT CAN POSSIBLY GO
HOPING IT WOULD HELP
DROWN OUT
THE VOICES IN MY HEAD

NO ONE LIKES YOU

        YOU AREN'T WORTH ANYTHING

            YOU DON'T DESERVE ANYTHING

                YOU CAN MAKE IT ALL DISAPPEAR

<u>END ME</u>

I BEGGED
I PRAYED
FOR IT ALL TO END
BUT NO ONE
WAS LISTENING

NO ONE CARES
ANYWAY

GOOD FRIENDS

I DON'T THINK IT'S THAT YOU FORGOT TO MESSAGE ME BACK
IT'S THAT YOU FORGOT I EVEN EXISTED
I THINK IT'S FINE IF YOU DON'T WANT TO WASTE ANYMORE OF
YOUR TIME
TRYING TO KEEP THIS FRIENDSHIP ALIVE IF YOU DIDN'T WANT IT
I WOULD LOVE IT IF YOU COULD STOP WASTING MY TIME AS WELL

LOVE MYSELF

I'VE ALWAYS STRUGGLED
WITH BEING ME
BECAUSE EITHER I KNEW
OR I'VE ALWAYS THOUGHT
THAT NO ONE LIKED
WHO I REALLY WAS

I CRIED ABOUT IT
FOR YEARS
PAST, PRESENT, AND PROBABLY FUTURE
BUT I DON'T NEED EVERYONE
TO LIKE WHO I AM
I JUST NEED ONE PERSON
TO LOVE WHO I AM

RELATIONSHIP PT. II

LIKE A GARDEN OF WILDFLOWERS
PEOPLE CAME TO PLANT THEIR SEED
BUT NO ONE STAYED AROUND
TO CARE FOR THEM
SO WEEDS TOOK OVER
DRAINING EVERYTHING FROM ME
BUT STILL, ONE FLOWER SPROUTED
ONLY BECAUSE I INVESTED
THE TIME AND EFFORT
WITH MYSELF

I HOPE YOU WERE ABLE TO FEEL
THE FEELINGS I'VE FELT
MAYBE YOU'VE PERSONALLY
HAD THESE FEELINGS
SO MAYBE WE'RE MORE
ALIKE THAN I THOUGHT –
MORE ALIKE
THAN *YOU* THOUGHT

WE MAY NOT
BE AS ALONE
AS WE ONCE THOUGHT

SOMETIMES IT'S DIFFICULT
FOR US TO DECIPHER OUR FEELINGS
LET ALONE FEEL LIKE WE HAVE TO
EXPLAIN THEM TO OTHERS

SOMETIMES WE WILL STRUGGLE
WITH THE SAME FEELINGS
OVER AND OVER AGAIN
AND THAT'S OK

SOMETIMES WE ARE FORCED TO BELIEVE
THAT WE HAVE TO ACT OR TO THINK A CERTAIN WAY
TO NOT SHOW ANY EMOTION
TO NOT TALK ABOUT WHAT WE'RE STRUGGLING WITH
BECAUSE IT MAKES US LOOK WEAK, SENSITIVE, DIFFERENT

BUT WE ALL *ARE* DIFFERENT

OUR JOURNEY

IS OUR STORY TO TELL

AND WE WILL TELL THOSE STORIES

WHEN WE'RE READY

PLEASE,
TAKE CARE OF YOURSELF

TO THOSE
WHO CAME TO LISTEN
THANKS
FOR CARING AND UNDERSTANDING

INDEX

#

1207 -181
5 -153
#WHYWESTAYSILENT -30

A

ABUSED -55
ADDICTED TO IT -173
AFRAID -51
ALIVE -69
ALWAYS ALONE -171
A MAN -13
ANTICIPATION -191
ARGUE -143
AWAKE -21

B

BAGGAGE -114
BAND-AID -83
BARE -207
BELIEVE -180
BLACKHOLE -67
BLOODLINE -145
BLOOD-STAINED -176
BLOOM -100
BORN TO SUFFER -135
BRAINWASHED -17
BREAKDOWN -45

BROKEN -49

C

CARE -178
CAREFREE -2
CATCH ME -132
CHANGE -3
CHILDHOOD THOUGHTS -8
CHOICE -80
CHOOSE -184
CYCLING FEELINGS -120

D

DARK SIDE OF THE MOON -97
DEAD -44
DESERVE -52
DID YOU KNOW -196
DIFFERENT -1
DISAPPEAR -39
DISAPPOINTMENT -4
DOES REALITY EQUAL TRUTH -134
DOMINO EFFECT -200
DON'T CROSS THE LINE -34
DON'T FORGET ME -177
DO YOU KNOW WHAT HAPPY IS -165
DRAG ME TO HELL -108
DREAMS -60
DREAMS PT.II -61
DROWNING -31
DROWN OUT -208

E

EASE -185

ELEMENTARY -6

END IT -98

END ME -209

EXCUSES -70

EXPECT -73

EXPLODE -78

EYES -64

F

FADE INTO DARKNESS -149

FAKE -103

FALL PT. I -46

FALL PT. II -48

FALLING DEEP -110

FAMILY -147

FAMILY VALUES -144

FOCUS -194

FOOL -32

FORGIVE -14

FOR GRANTED -190

FUTURE -112

G

GENUINE -91

GREY -186

GROWING UP -195

GROWTH -126

GOAL -206

GO BACK -43
GOODBYE -162
GOOD FRIENDS -210

H

HAPPY MASK -130
HARD TO LOVE -117
HEAL -175
HEART -53
HELP ME -141
HERE -128
HIDE -77
HIGH HOPES -166
HOPE -123
HOW DO YOU KNOW -170
HOW TO FEEL -50

I

I AM HAPPY THOUGH, AT TIMES -159
I CAN'T REMEMBER -93
I DECIDE MY FATE -158
I DESERVE IT -92
I GIVE UP -124
I HOPE YOU CARED -150
I MISS -137
I'M HURT -157
I'M SCARED -155
I'M TIRED -88
I'M TIRED PT. II -167
INCOMPLETE -187

I NEED YOU -142
IT'S TOO LATE -156

J
JOKER -16
JUMP -19
JUST BE HAPPY -160
JUST THOUGHT YOU SHOULD KNOW -189

K
KARMA -79
KILL -111
KNOW -104

L
LEARN -205
LEAVE ME ALONE -139
LIFES A GAMBLE -203
LIKE ME -74
LOCKED OUT -113
LOOK AT YOURSELF -152
LOOKING -56
LOST -10
LOVE MYSELF -211

M
MAGIC -87
MASK -71
MATTER -76
MD -25

ME -59
MENTAL -40
MISSING -41
MY APOLOGIES -26
MY WORLD IS CRUMBLING -169

N

NEGATIVE -63
NEVER AGAIN -198
NEVER LET GO -129
NO EYES, EARS, NOSE, MOUTH, OR FEELINGS -23
NOTHING WORKS OUT -58

O

OBLIVIOUS -102
OK PT. I -94
OK PT. II -95
ONE OF THOSE -84
OPEN UP -82
OPPO PT. I -182
OPPO PT. II -183

P

PAINFUL -125
PAINFUL WORDS -168
PARALYSIS -22
PESSIMIST -62
PIERCED -72
PIERCER -131
PLAYED -36

PLEASE LIKE ME -138
PRETEND -68
PROBLEMS -151
PROVE -7

R
RELATIONSHIP -105
RELATIONSHIP PT. II -212
REMEMBER -42
REPRESS -154
RISK -66
ROSE -99
RUINED -20
RUN -96

S
SAFE HAVEN -11
SCARED -38
SCARS -116
SECRETS -65
SELF-AWARE -86
SELF-CENTERED -85
SELFISH -5
SELF-WORTH -174
SEXUAL ORIENTATION -197
SHARE -121
SIBLING -146
SILENCE -192
SMILE -106
START OVER -109

STONE COLD -18
STUCK INBETWEEN -122
SUMMER NIGHTS -12
SUN -115
SUN PT. II -193

T
TAKE MY LIFE -163
TEARS -136
TEENAGE THOUGHTS -15
TEMPORARY -199
TERRIFIED -9
THANKS, I HOPE -119
THE END -164
THE PATH ENOURAGED -148
THIRD CHANCES -28
TOUCH -140
TRAPPED -54
TRUST -188

U
UGLY -75
UNCONTROLLABLE -172
UNDERSTAND ME -107
UNHAPPY -101
UNILATERAL -27
UNSATISFIED -90

<u>V</u>
VOID -89
VULNERABLE -81

<u>W</u>
WATCH OUT -127
WE NEED HELP, I NEED HELP -161
WHAT ACTUALLY MATTERS -204
WHAT IS REALITY -133
WHAT I WANTED -201
WHO AM I -57
WORRY -33
WORTHY -118

<u>X</u>
XX -29

<u>Y</u>
YOU DON'T KNOW WHAT TO DO -202
YOU KNOW I KNOW -179
YOU'LL NEVER FORGET -24

JUST THOUGHT YOU SHOULD KNOW

COPYRIGHT © 2019 BY THOMAS TRENH. ALL RIGHTS RESERVED. NO PART
OF THIS BOOK MAY BE USED OR REPRODUCED IN ANY MATTER WITHOUT
WRITTEN PERMISSION.

ISBN: 9781070437538

THOMASTRENH.COM
TWITTER @THOMASTRENH
INSTAGRAM @STORYOFTHOMAST

Manufactured by Amazon.ca
Bolton, ON

14838371R00133